This Book Belongs To:

Dennis M.

Melissa Miller

W9-BSQ-471

The Rand McNally Book of
Favorite
Bible Stories and Verses

by Mary Alice Jones

Rand McNally & Company   Chicago · Established 1856

This book consists of A STORY ABOUT JESUS, copyrighted ©
MCMLIII by Rand McNally & Company under the title *My First
Book About Jesus*, BIBLE STORIES Old Testament, THE TEN
COMMANDMENTS for Children, PRAYERS AND GRACES for
a Small Child, copyrighted © by Rand McNally & Company in
MCMLIV, MCMLVI, and MCMLV respectively. 1979 Edition.
Printed in U.S.A.

Library of Congress Catalog Card Number: 63-11274

CONTENTS

A STORY ABOUT JESUS

Long ago there lived on earth a man
whose name was Jesus.
God sent him to earth to help people.

Jesus was a carpenter.

He made things people needed.

He made them good and strong and sturdy.

Sometimes children played outside the carpenter shop.

Jesus liked to watch them play.

One day Jesus was walking with some friends.
They stopped at a farm.

Jesus said, "The farmer plants the seed.
The seed grows. First a green stem comes up.
It becomes a stalk, heavy with grain.
And all of you are fed.
This is the way God planned it."

One day a sad man came to Jesus.

"My son is very sick," he said.

"Will you help him get well?"

Jesus said, "I will help him. God will show me how.

Your son will get better." And the boy did get well.

Many people came to Jesus.

He needed some helpers.

He asked some fishermen to leave their boats
    and go with him.

The fishermen became Jesus' first helpers.

Jesus liked to have children come to see him.
He told his helpers, "Let the children come to me.
Never tell them I am too busy to see them.
God loves them, every one.
And I love them."

Jesus taught people.

"God wants you to be good to each other," he said.

"If you have two coats and someone else has no coat, give one of your coats to him.

This is God's plan for you.

This is the way to be happy."

Jesus often told the people stories.
He told a story about a lamb and a shepherd.
A little lamb got lost. Night came.
The little lamb was frightened.

The good shepherd looked and looked
   for the little lamb.
And by-and-by he found it. He took it home again.
The little lamb was glad. The shepherd was glad.

Once Jesus and his friends were in a boat
out on the water.
A storm came up. The friends were afraid.

Jesus said, "Why are you afraid?
God is with you in the storm.
See, the waves are growing still."
So his friends went to work and brought the boat
    to shore.

There was a man who had been unfair.

He had taken more than his share.

Jesus came to see the man. Jesus was friendly.

The man was ashamed of being unfair.

He said, "I will give back all I have taken unfairly."

Often Jesus talked with God.
He loved God. He knew God loved him.
He knew God was helping him every day.
He knew he was God's son.

Jesus taught people about God.
He said, "Look at the bright flowers
and the flying birds.
God takes care of them.

"He loves you much more. Each one of you.
He sends you good gifts of food
    and sunshine and rain.
He helps you when you are lonely or sick or bad."

Once when Jesus was on a trip,
    people had a parade for him.
They brought a donkey for him to ride.
The people marched along waving green branches.

They sang songs of praise.

They wanted to tell Jesus that they loved him.

They wanted to tell God they were glad
Jesus had come.

There were some men who thought God loved them more than he loved other people.
They turned against Jesus. They hurt him.

But unfriendly men could not get rid of Jesus!
Because what Jesus taught about God was true.
And God was with him.
So Jesus has gone on helping everybody.

Joseph Goes on an Errand

Joseph lived in a large family. He had ten big brothers and one little brother.

Now, Joseph's father had many, many sheep. His sons helped him take care of them. When there was grass and water near their father's tents, Joseph went with his big brothers to feed and water the sheep. But sometimes the sheep had to be taken far from home to find enough grass and water.

These long trips took many days, and only the big brothers went along. Joseph wanted to go but he knew he must wait until his father told him he was big enough. So he stayed near his father's tents with his little brother.

One time the big brothers were away days and days. Joseph knew his father was worried.

Then early one morning his father called Joseph. "Your brothers have been gone a long time. They are feeding the flocks near Shechem.

You are big enough, now, to go on an errand away from home. You know how to get to Shechem. Go and find your brothers and see how they are getting along so that I may have word of them."

Joseph was glad his father thought he was big enough to go on an errand by himself.

"Yes, Father, I will go for you. I will start right away."

So Joseph started toward Shechem. He walked and walked. It was hot. He grew tired. Finally, he came to Shechem. Then he looked and looked. But he could not find his brothers.

A man saw the boy wandering about the fields.

"Whom are you looking for?" he asked.

"I am looking for my brothers who are feeding our father's flocks. But I cannot find them."

"I know where they are," the man told Joseph. "They left here a few days ago. I heard them say, 'Let us go to Dothan.'"

The man showed Joseph the way to Dothan, and on and on Joseph went.

By and by he came to Dothan. The man was right! His brothers had come to Dothan. Joseph saw them, and he saw the sheep eating grass on the hillside.

So Joseph found his brothers. As he ran forward to meet them, Joseph was feeling proud of having done the errand his father had asked him to do.

Miriam and Her Baby Brother

Once there was a wicked king. He did not like some of the people in his country. So he passed a law to hurt them. The law said that whenever a baby boy was born to them, the baby should be taken away.

In one family there was a girl whose name was Miriam. Then a baby brother was born.

"Oh, Mother, we must think of a way to hide our baby," Miriam said.

So Miriam and her mother thought and thought.

"We will make a little cradle boat, snug and tight so the water can't get in," the mother said. "Then we will wrap the baby in a blanket and put the little cradle boat in the tall grass at the edge of the river."

Miriam clapped her hands. "What a wonder-

ful plan, Mother! No one will think of looking there! And if the baby cries, no one can hear him."

Quickly Miriam and her mother carried out their plan. Then Miriam said, "I will hide here on the river bank to watch the baby."

Everything was quiet. Then Miriam heard voices. Peeping out from the tall grass, she saw the princess, the daughter of the wicked king. And the princess had seen the cradle boat!

"What is that?" she asked one of the girls with her. "Go and bring it to me."

While Miriam trembled, the girl brought the little cradle boat from the river. The princess moved the blanket and saw the baby cuddled inside. And the baby cried.

"What a dear baby!" the princess said. Then her face grew sad as she remembered the wicked law. "Some mother is trying to hide her baby," she whispered.

Then the princess spoke again. "I will adopt this baby myself. No one will dare take him away when I say he is the son of the princess."

Miriam ran out from the high grasses. She had a plan! "The princess is too young to take care of a baby," she began politely. "I know a good nurse."

The princess smiled. "Bring the good nurse to me," she said.

So Miriam ran to her own home. She told her mother all that had happened. And the mother hurried to the princess.

"I have found this baby near the river's edge," the princess explained. "I am going to adopt him as my own. And I am going to name him Moses. But I need a good nurse. Will you take care of the baby for me?"

And so the baby's own mother took care of the baby Moses. And the baby grew and was safe and happy.

Ruth and Naomi

Ruth was a stranger in the town of Bethlehem. She had come from her own country to take care of her mother-in-law Naomi. For Naomi was old, and Ruth loved her very much.

Now, Ruth and Naomi were poor. They had no money to buy food.

Early one morning Ruth went to the fields where the young men and women of Bethlehem were working to gather the ripe grain. She spoke timidly to the man in charge. "Please," she said, "may I gather the fallen grain in the fields?"

The man had heard that Ruth had come to Bethlehem to take care of Naomi. So he spoke kindly to her. "Yes, you may glean. Watch the other girls and do as they do."

So Ruth began to gather the grain. All morning she worked, without resting even for a moment. About noon Boaz, the owner of the field, came. He, too, spoke kindly to Ruth.

"Stop working now and then," he told her, "and drink the water which the young men have drawn. And when mealtime comes, eat with the others."

"You are very kind to me, a stranger," Ruth answered.

Boaz spoke again. "I have heard all that you have done for your mother-in-law Naomi. May God help you and comfort you."

When mealtime came, Ruth went in to eat. As she ate the good food, she thought of Naomi at home with so little to eat. "They have given me more food than I need," she said to herself. "I will save some of my portion and take it home to Naomi."

Then Ruth went back to the fields and worked all afternoon.

When the day's work was done, she hurried

home. "See," she called to Naomi, "see the good grain I worked for!" And she poured the grain into the vessel Naomi had ready.

Then she brought out her surprise. "And, see, I saved some of the good lunch they gave me. I saved it for you."

So Ruth and Naomi had food for supper that night. And they had food for supper every night. Because Boaz had told Ruth that she could glean in his field every day.

David and the Sheep

David was a shepherd. He took care of his father's sheep.

Many boys would have been lonely. The place where the sheep were kept was far from the town. Many times David stayed all night in the hills with only the sheep for company.

But David was not lonely. The sunrise and the sunset and the clouds and the brooks and the stars at night made him feel close to God. Often he made up poems about the things he saw about him. He had a little harp and he played happy tunes. Sometimes he made tunes for the poems he had written and he would sing them as songs of praise to God.

David's job was to take care of the sheep. He looked for good grass for his flock. He found pools of water where it was safe for his sheep to drink. And when the sun was hot, he led them to shady places to rest.

One night David was making soft music on his little harp. The sheep were all about him, fast asleep. Suddenly David saw a shadow move. It was not the shadow of a restless sheep. It was not the shadow of a tree moved by the night breeze. It was the shadow of a lion! And the lion was moving toward a little lamb.

David laid his harp on a rock. His feet seemed not to touch the ground so swiftly did he move toward the lamb. The lion was very near. But David was nearer! He reached the little lamb and lifted him into the shelter of his arms. Then

he reached for a large piece of rock and turned toward the lion.

The great beast seemed to know that David was not afraid of him. He seemed to know that David was not going to let him get near any of his sheep. As the rock came flying toward him, the lion gave a parting roar and dashed away into the night.

The sheep waked up. They ran about, frightened. Then they heard David's voice, speaking to them. It was the voice they trusted. They stopped running around.

As the sheep became quiet, David put the little lamb back in the flock. Then he picked up his harp and began playing soft tunes. The sheep felt safe now. They knew their shepherd was taking care of them. And soon they were all asleep again.

THE TEN COMMANDMENTS
for Children

Thou shalt have no other gods before me.

Exodus 20:1-3

GOD IS VERY GREAT and very good.

Men and women and boys and girls who think of God know that they must not put what they want before what God wants. They know that they must want to do what God wants them to do. They must put nothing before that.

For God is very great and very good.

Thou shalt not make unto thee any graven image.

Exodus 20:4-5

IN OLDEN TIMES men and women sometimes made images of wood and stone and thought these images could help them if they prayed to them. But God was working in the world. By and by the people listened when God spoke to them. By and by they learned that only God could hear them.

We know that only God can hear us when we pray. We know, too, that God always does hear us and helps us.

Thou shalt not take the name of the Lord thy God in vain.

Exodus 20:7

THE GREAT GOD, the Creator of the heavens and the earth, is the holy one. Men do not speak of him carelessly. They speak of him reverently. They speak of him lovingly. For God is very great, and God is very good. The heavens declare his glory, and all the inhabitants of the earth stand in awe of him. He makes light to shine out of darkness and tells the number of the stars. He heals the broken-hearted and is mindful of all his children. He is *God*. His name is holy.

Remember the sabbath day, to keep it holy.

Exodus 20:8-10

IN THE PLAN OF GOD for man's happiness is a place for quiet and rest and worship. To help God's children think of him and talk with him, there is a special day. In the Bible it is called the sabbath. On this day men and women do not go to work. Boys and girls do not go to school. They go to church to sing and pray and think together of God's plan for them and for all men everywhere.

honor
thy father
and thy mother.

Exodus 20:12

IN THE FAMILY mothers and fathers help their children in many, many ways, long before the children can understand about it or can say, "Thank you." As the children grow older, they do many things for their fathers and mothers. Mothers and fathers and boys and girls help one another, not because they must, but because they love one another. Boys and girls remember to do what their parents ask them to do because they know their parents want what is best for their children. Though their parents sometimes make mistakes, boys and girls know that their parents are wiser than they are. And so they show respect to their parents and trust them.

Thou shalt not kill.

Exodus 20:13

GOD ONLY IS GREAT ENOUGH to make life. No man can make even the tiniest seed or blade of grass or flying bird. But God, the Creator, gives life to all creatures. "It is he that hath made us, and not we ourselves." God tells his children that life is very precious. Because he has given us life, it is God's plan that each one of his children should live happily, without fear that his neighbor will take away his life. It is God's plan that each one of his children should help take care of the life of all his other children. Life is the gift of God. It is sacred.

Thou shalt not commit adultery.

Exodus 20:14

IT IS THE PLAN OF GOD that his children live in families. It is his plan that a man and a woman should love one another and make a home together and rear children. The father and mother and children have other friends, whom they like and enjoy. But the members of the family care for one another more than for any other friends. The happiness of each member of the family is important to every other member of the family. Fathers and mothers who truly love one another and truly love their children are God's best helpers. For they are carrying out God's plan that a man and a woman love each other and rear children. This is God's plan for a happy world.

Thou shalt not steal.

Exodus 20:15

BECAUSE GOD LOVES ALL his children, he wants his children to share with one another. If one is hungry or cold, it is God's plan that someone else should help him have clothes and a house to live in and food to eat. If one keeps more than his share, he is not carrying out God's plan. Also, if one takes away what belongs to someone else, he is breaking God's law. It is right that any man or woman or boy or girl who really needs something should *ask* for it. But it is wrong for any person to *take* what he wants. To refuse to share with someone who is in need, and to take what is not one's own—both make people unhappy.

Thou shalt not bear false witness against thy neighbor.

Exodus 20:16

TO TELL the *good* one knows about someone else may help him. To tell of something bad which the person has done may hurt him. But to say he has done something bad which he has not really done is very sure to hurt him.

Often it is easy to blame someone else for an accident. Sometimes it is easy, even, to blame someone else for one's own carelessness. And once in a while there is a boy or girl who does something he knows is wrong. When harm comes from it, he says someone else did it. That, God tells us, is sinful.

Thou shalt not covet.

Exodus 20:17

IT IS EASY TO WANT something which someone else has. But God tells us that it does not make us happy to think about what someone else has and to wish it were ours. It is better to think of the good things we have and to enjoy them and share them with others. If we really need something more than we have, we may ask God to help us to work and to plan wisely. For God loves us and knows all the things we have need of.

The Ten Great Words

THE GREAT LAWS which came to be known as the Ten Great Words, or the Ten Commandments, were very precious to the men of olden times. By and by they came to be written. The people took very good care of them. Often they failed to obey them, but always they came back to them and knew they were *good* laws. And through all the years, from those days to the present time, the Ten Commandments have helped people to know the law of God.

In the Bible there is a wonderful story about this great set of laws. It is the story about how these laws came to be known to the people. The story shows how much the people believed in these laws, how important they thought the laws were. It shows that the people knew the laws were, indeed, the laws of God.

In our Bible these great laws have been kept for us. You can find them and read them for yourself. They are in the book called Exodus, the second book in the Bible. You will find them in the twentieth chapter of this book, that is, in Exodus 20:1–17.

The Story of the Ten Commandments

SHALL we always be slaves?" the people asked.

It was long, long ago. The people called the Israelites had been living in Egypt for many years. But then there came a king of Egypt who feared the Israelites lest they become too powerful. He passed cruel laws against them. The people became slaves, working early and late at hard labor for the king.

Now there lived in the palace a young Israelite who was the adopted son of the king's daughter. His name was Moses. He lived a life of ease as a prince of Egypt.

One day Moses was watching the Israelites work. He saw them driven with great whips. Then Moses remembered that he, too, was an Israelite. These were his people.

He became very angry. He fought one of the Egyptian officers. Then he ran away and hid in the desert.

In the long nights under the desert stars Moses thought of his people. He thought of the God of the Israelites, of whom he had been taught by his nurse. And one day, in the quiet of the desert, God spoke to Moses.

"I have seen the afflictions of my people in Egypt and have heard their cry. And I will deliver my people and bring them unto a good land." As Moses listened in awe, God continued. "I will send you into Egypt, that you may bring forth my people out of slavery."

Now Moses was frightened. "Who am I that I should lead forth the people out of Egypt?" he asked.

God spoke again. "Certainly I will be with you."

And so Moses went back to Egypt. He worked quietly among the Israelites. He told them that God had promised to free his people from the Egyptians.

The people listened to Moses. They made plans to escape. It took a long time. But finally one night they slipped away into the wilderness.

The journey was long. But the travelers did not stop. God was leading them to a new country, a land where they could live free from slavery.

"It will be a beautiful country," a mother said to her tired child. "There will be milk for you, and fruit, and sweet honey for your bread."

The people went on and on. Food and water were scarce. The people became discouraged and began to grumble.

"This is as bad as being a slave in Egypt."

"Did Moses bring us to the wilderness to die?"

"Has God forgotten his promise to help us?"

Moses heard the grumblings of the people. He called them together. "Here at the foot of Mount Sinai let us make camp," he said. "And we will pray to God."

So they made camp. And Moses prayed to God. And God answered Moses and comforted him.

Then Moses spoke to the people. "God is with us. He has promised to show us the way into a new country. He says to you now, 'If you will keep my commandments, then you shall be my own people.'"

The people were encouraged by the words of Moses.

But Moses knew that the people needed something to remind them always of the presence of God and of the laws of God. He wanted to be a good leader. So Moses went away by himself, up the lonely slopes of Mount Sinai. There he stayed many days and nights. He asked God to help him know how God wanted the people to live. Then he felt he knew. God himself had taught him the laws which would enable the people to be happy and good.

Then Moses found two smooth stones. And on the

stones the laws of God were written.

Moses came down from the mountain. He called all the people together and held up the stones on which the laws of God were written. He said, "These are the words which the Lord has commanded, that you should do them."

Then there came over Mount Sinai a heavy cloud. Bright lightning flashed through the cloud, and there was a mighty roaring of thunder. The people said, "It is the Lord." And they bowed themselves to the ground and worshiped. And they said to Moses, "All that the Lord has spoken unto us, that we will do."

Then Moses told the people to make a big tent, which

was to be their church, and to make an ark, or chest, and to put the ark in the center of the tent.

Soon the tent church was finished. In the center of the tent stood the ark, overlaid with gold, the gift of all the people. And Moses put into the ark the tablets of stone on which were written the laws of God.

The people carried their tent church with them as they traveled on. By and by they came to the new country.

The years passed. The people became a nation. In the capital city the king built a beautiful temple. And in the central place stood the ark containing the tablets of stone on which the laws of God were recorded.

And from that day to this people around the world learn these laws of God, called the Ten Commandments.

PRAYERS AND GRACES
for a Small Child

WHEN I WAKE UP

Out of my window
    My yard looks so gay!
I feel God is near me,
    And so I will pray.

MORNING SONG

Early in the morning
    I sing a happy song:
"God will be my helper,
    All this whole day long!"

THANK YOU

Thank you, dear God,
   For sleep through the night;
Thank you, dear God,
   For the glad morning light.

IN THE MORNING

In the morning, in the morning,
In the morning comes the sun!
In the morning, in the morning,
I am glad the day's begun!
In the morning, in the morning,
Pray, "God bless us, every one!"

GOD'S LOVE

Thank you, God, that I can feel
Your love about me all this day.

HELP ME TODAY

Dear God, please help me to say
Kind words to all my friends today;
Dear God, please help me to play
With all my friends in a happy way.

FOR EYES TO SEE

Thank you, God, for eyes to see
A river and a tree,
A baby kitten that's so wee,
And my mother's face as she looks at me.

GRACE

God is great
    And God is good;
Let us thank him
    For our food.

THANK YOU, GOD

Thank you, God,
For milk and bread
And other things so good;
Thank you, God,
For those who help
To grow and cook our food.

Elizabeth McE. Shields

HAPPY THOUGHTS

I'm glad, I'm glad, I'm glad today!
I'm glad that I can run and play.
  I'm glad that I can see the sky,
  I'm glad that I can swing up high.
I'm glad, I'm glad, I'm glad today!
I'm glad, dear God! That's how I pray.

TO BE A HELPER

My mother and my daddy
    Work hard for me and are kind.
I want to help them, too, dear God,
    In every way I can find.

KIND PEOPLE

I thought about the carpenter
Who made our house snug and warm;

I thought about the farmer
Who grows our food on his farm;

I thought about kind people
Who work for us each day.

And then I thought of thanking God—
And that is how I pray.

FOR THE GOOD WORLD

Thank you, dear God,
For the good world you have planned:
For rain and wind and snowflakes;

For trees and grass and flowers;
For birds and pets and horses;

For books and music and pictures;
For home and school and church.
Thank you, dear God,
For the good world you have planned.

FOR LOVING ME

Thank you, dear God, for loving me
   When I do the things I should;
Thank you, God, for loving me
   Even when I am not good.
Thank you, God, for loving me.

ON A STORMY NIGHT

The thunder is noisier than I like,
And the lightning is very bright.
Help me, God, to feel you near
On a windy and stormy night.

I THINK OF GOD AND MOTHER

I think God is like my mother:
    She helps me the whole day through,
And comforts me when I'm sorry,
    And loves me whatever I do.

I THINK OF GOD AND DADDY

I think God is like my daddy:
    I'm not afraid when he's near.
He knows how to answer my questions,
    And he's never too busy to hear.

A HAPPY DAY

It's been a happy day, dear God.
I helped my mother bake a cake
And played with Mary on the swing
And watched the ducks swim on the lake.
It's been a happy day, dear God.

GOOD NIGHT

Good night, good night, good night
To friendly helpers everywhere.
God help you all,
God bless you all,
And keep you in his loving care.

THANK GOD FOR NIGHT

Thank you, God, for the night—
For the shining stars
And the quiet dark,
For my own little bed
And for rest and sleep.
Thank you, God, for the night.

THANKS FOR CARE

I thank you for your care, dear God,
Before I go to sleep,
And send my love all 'round my block
To all the people in your keep.

OFF TO SLEEP

I've had my good-night kiss and hug,
And now I'm all tucked in and snug.
Good night, dear God,
I'm going to sleep.
I know that you are near.